# Zion National Park

## Attractions & Sights to See

Billy Grinslott & Kinsey Marie Books

ISBN - 9781960612991

Hwy 9 is the major road providing access to Zion National Park. It winds past the park visitor center and museum, and past many famous Zion landmarks. At any time of the year, you can drive through Zion National Park and the Zion-Mount Carmel Tunnel on State highway 9. Parking is limited along this road, but the views are incredible. It's a great drive, but it does not go into the park where the activities are.

Zion Canyon Scenic Drive. From March through late November, access to the Zion Canyon Scenic Drive inside Zion Park is by shuttle bus only. Private vehicles are allowed only when the Shuttle is not in operation. Bicycles are allowed on the Zion Canyon Scenic Drive, check with the park first. Zion Canyon Scenic Drive is approximately 7 miles long. The entire round-trip ride takes about an hour and a half. It stops at a few sightseeing opportunities.

The Narrows is the narrowest section of Zion Canyon. It has walls a thousand feet tall and the river sometimes just twenty to thirty feet wide, is one of the most popular areas in Zion National Park. A hike through the Narrows requires hiking in the Virgin River. You must get your feet wet since there is no trail.

Angel's Landing requires permits to take this hike. You must apply to a lottery system. It is one of the more popular hikes at Zion. But it is also dangerous. You are climbing 1,488 feet in elevation, up steep switchbacks. The part of the trail is along an exposed ridge, it is narrow and has chains to hang on too. As you can see in the lower right of the picture. This hike will test your fear of heights.

Canyon Overlook Trail is a moderate, 1 mile trail on the East side of Zion. The path begins with a series of sandstone steps with a metal handrails leading visitors over rocky terrain above a canyon. Near the end of the trail, the view opens to an expansive view of the canyon. At the end of the trail is a fenced cliff edge facing the main Zion Canyon, with excellent views of the Towers of the Virgin. Keep an eye out for bighorn sheep along the trail.

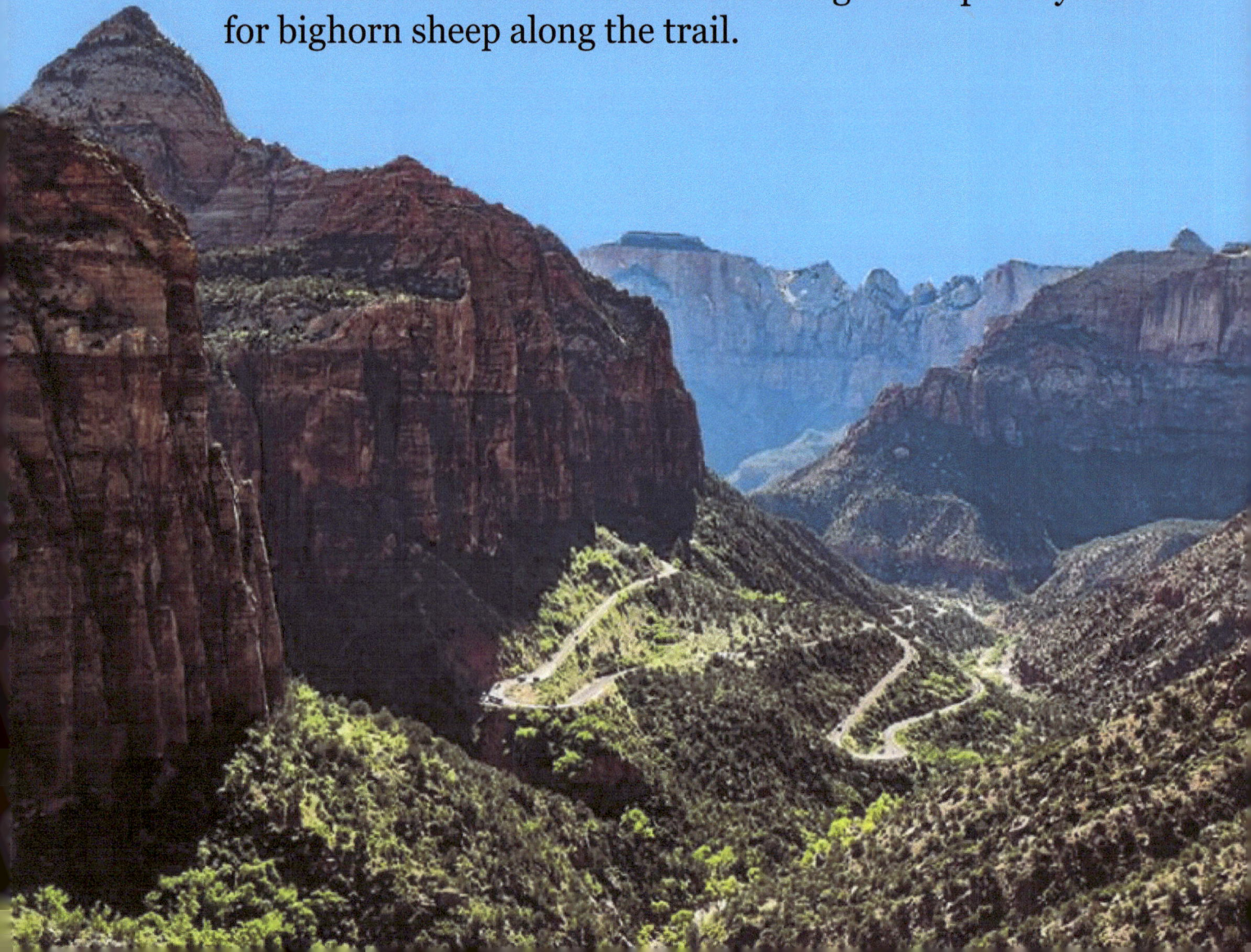

Observation Trail and Point. This short canyon leads hikers to the junction between the Observation Point Trail and the East Rim Trail. It is a narrow canyon, 1,100 feet above the Floor of the Valley Road. The trail follows along a shelf above the canyon floor. Below the trail, the canyon drops into an extremely narrow slot, which is a challenging technical route. A permit is required to descend Echo Canyon.

Zion Canyon is the most visited part of Zion and offers easy, moderate, and strenuous hikes. Most Zion Canyon hikes are accessible only by the park shuttle from March through November and require stopping at the appropriate shuttle stop. Be sure to check the shuttle schedule prior to starting your trip and arrive early to find parking

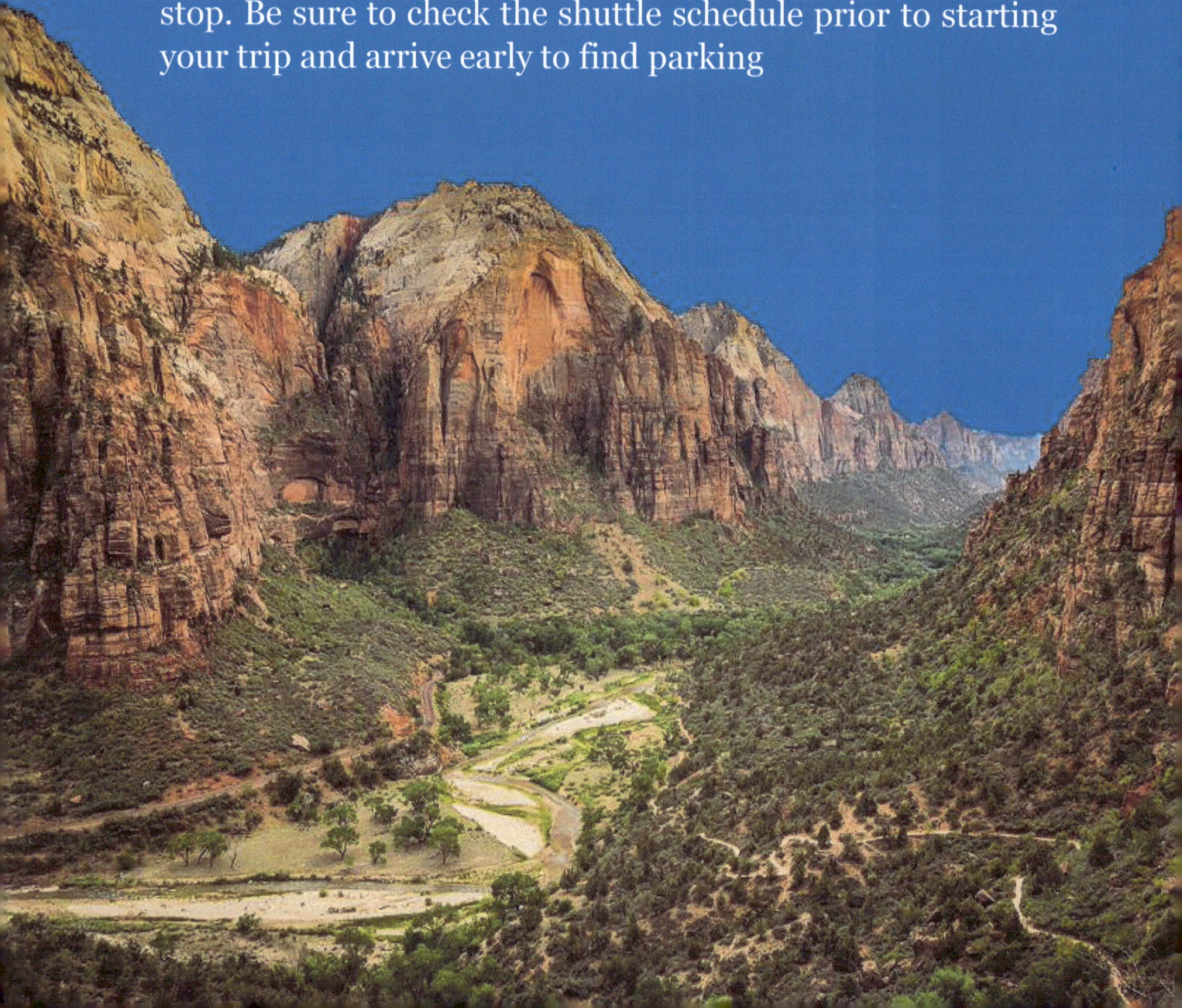

Canyon Junction Bridge. Access to the Canyon Junction Bridge in Zion National Park, take the Pa'rus trail leading from the Visitor Center. This bridge offers a great view of the mighty Watchman Mountain. This viewpoint is most popular at sunset. The bridge crosses the river and has great views all around.

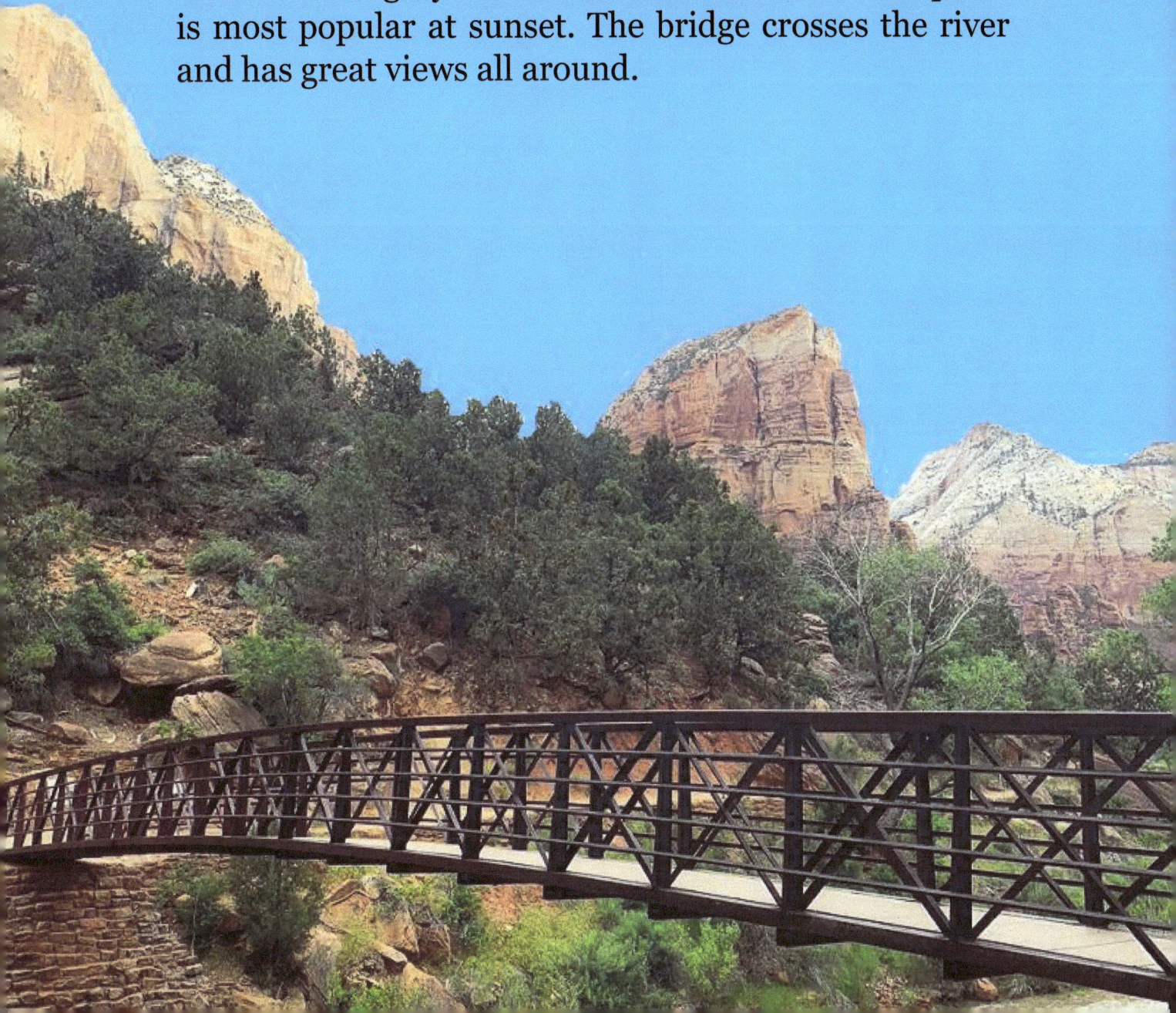

Weeping Rock is called that because water consistently runs out of the walls. Short but steep. From the parking area, you'll cross the bridge and head to the left onto a paved trail to Weeping Rock. The trail ends at a set of steps leading you to a rock alcove with dripping springs.

Kolob Canyon Road. A five-mile drive along the Kolob Canyons Road allows visitors to view the cliffs. It has access to other trails and scenic viewpoints. Located northwest of the Zion Canyon Visitor Center, Kolob Canyons is easily accessed off Interstate 15. It's well worth the trip.

Kolob Terrace Road. This is one of the best things to do in Zion National Park. Views from all sides of the car are amazing. There are plenty of areas to pull off and appreciate the park. Lava point is a breathtaking overlook, and there is plenty of space to have a picnic. Kolob Terrace Road runs from Virgin, Utah to Kolob Reservoir. The entire point-to-point route is about 25 miles.

The Kolob Canyons are a unique area of Zion National Park. It offers huge peaks of sandstone, canyon streams and cascading falls. It has over 20 miles of hiking trails. Kolob Canyon is home to one of the longest natural arches in the world. The Kolob Canyons are located at Exit 40 on Interstate 15, 17 miles south of Cedar City.

Zion-Mt. Carmel Highway. This scenic drive is worth it. If you drive from the canyon junction to the east, when you pass through the Zion-Mount Carmel tunnel (1.1 miles), you reach the trail head of Canyon overlook trail, you may hike the trail if you have time, otherwise, you can continue to drive the scenic drive. This 26-mile road winds its way eastward through some of the most exceptional terrain in the world.

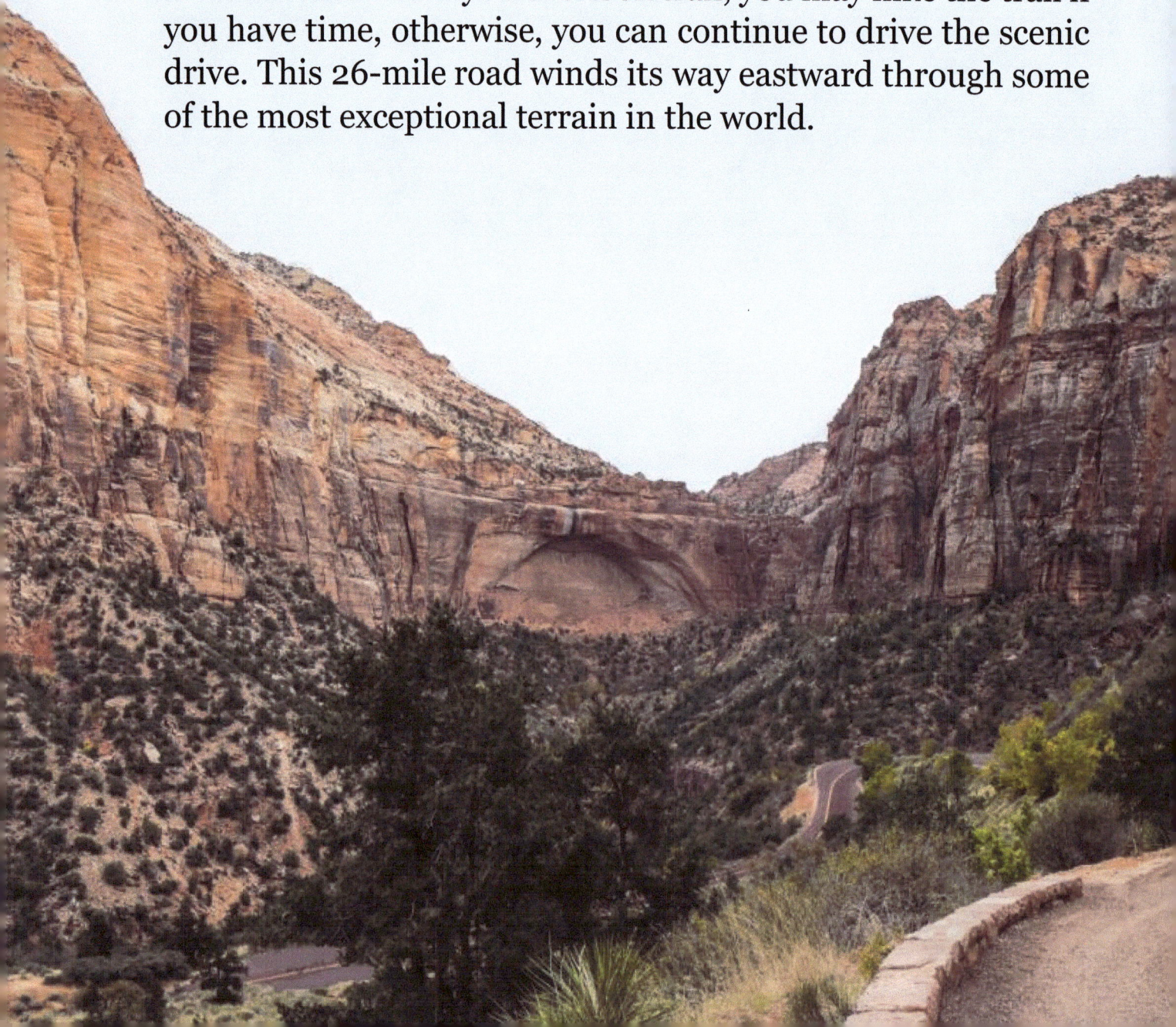

The Riverside Walk is a relatively flat and paved 2.2-mile round-trip trail in the northern end of Zion Canyon. This easy walking trail follows the Virgin River as the tall cliff walls narrow in around you. The Riverside Walk is mostly flat through the first half-mile, although paving is irregular in some sections and minor drop-offs are present.

The Temple of Sinawava was carved by the Virgin River's incredible flow and power. To access this area, take the riverside walk trail ending at the Zion Narrows. Just one mile in length and paved over the entire route. The walk is as easy as a sidewalk stroll, making it perfect for everyone.

The Watchman Trail is a moderate out-and-back hike accessed from the Zion Canyon Visitor Center. If you climb up on watchman you will have a magnificent viewpoint of the Watchman, Temples and Towers, lower Zion Canyon, and the Town of Springdale. Watchman trail is 3.3 miles roundtrip.

The Subway is not for beginners. It is a technical slot canyon hike. To complete the hike, you wade, swim, scramble, and climb down the Left Fork of North Creek. The stream is the trail for most of the route. Some of the holes are deep enough that you have to swim, and the water is cold.

The Pa'rus Trail follows the Virgin River and has some of the best views of the Watchman. It is accessible for wheelchairs, pets on leashes, and bicycles. Along the way, the scenery is quite pleasant, including several bridges that cross above the river, various wildflowers, and mule deer can be spotted.

Court of the Patriarchs. Enjoy spectacular views of the three patriarchs, Abraham, Isaac, and Jacob. The three peaks are best seen from an overlook on the east side of the Zion Canyon Scenic Drive. The trail to the overlook is very short but steep. Also at this location you can enjoy excellent views of the Sentinel and Mount Moroni.

There are three Emerald Pools. Upper, Middle, and Lower in Zion National Park. Visitors may choose from as many trails: a short, 1.2-mile round-trip loop to the Lower Pool. A 2-mile round-trip visit to the Middle and Lower Pools. A 2.5-mile round-trip hike to all three. All Emerald Pool hikes lead to sparkling waterfalls and glistening pools.

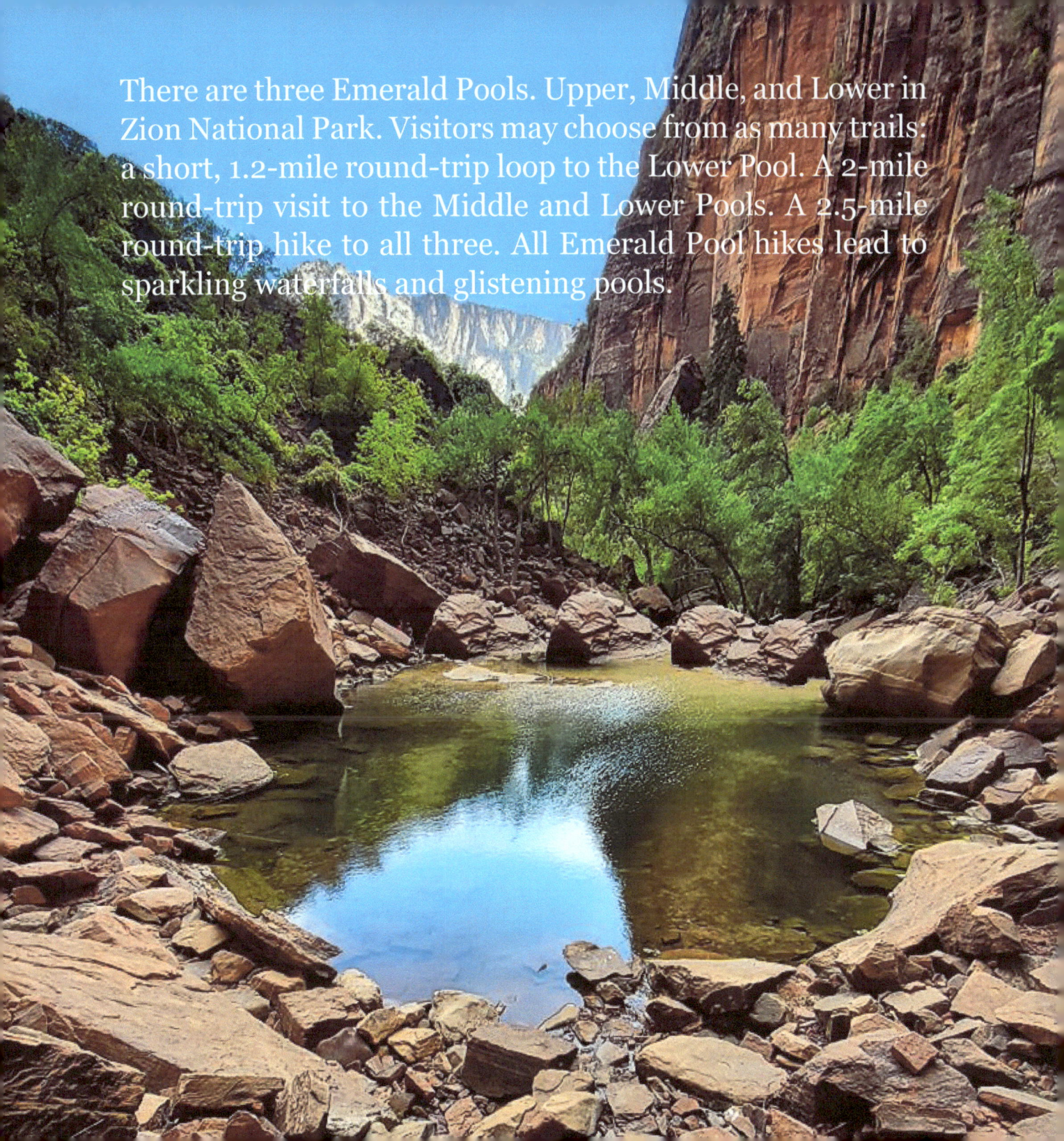

Taylor Creek, or Middle Taylor Creek, is a scenic hike in the Kolob Section of Zion National Park. The hike visits two historic cabins, as well as a deep walled canyon. The hike is very exposed to the sun to the first cabin, then gets a bit more shaded. The hike into the canyon is just over 2.5 miles long, rising just under 500 feet in elevation along its route.

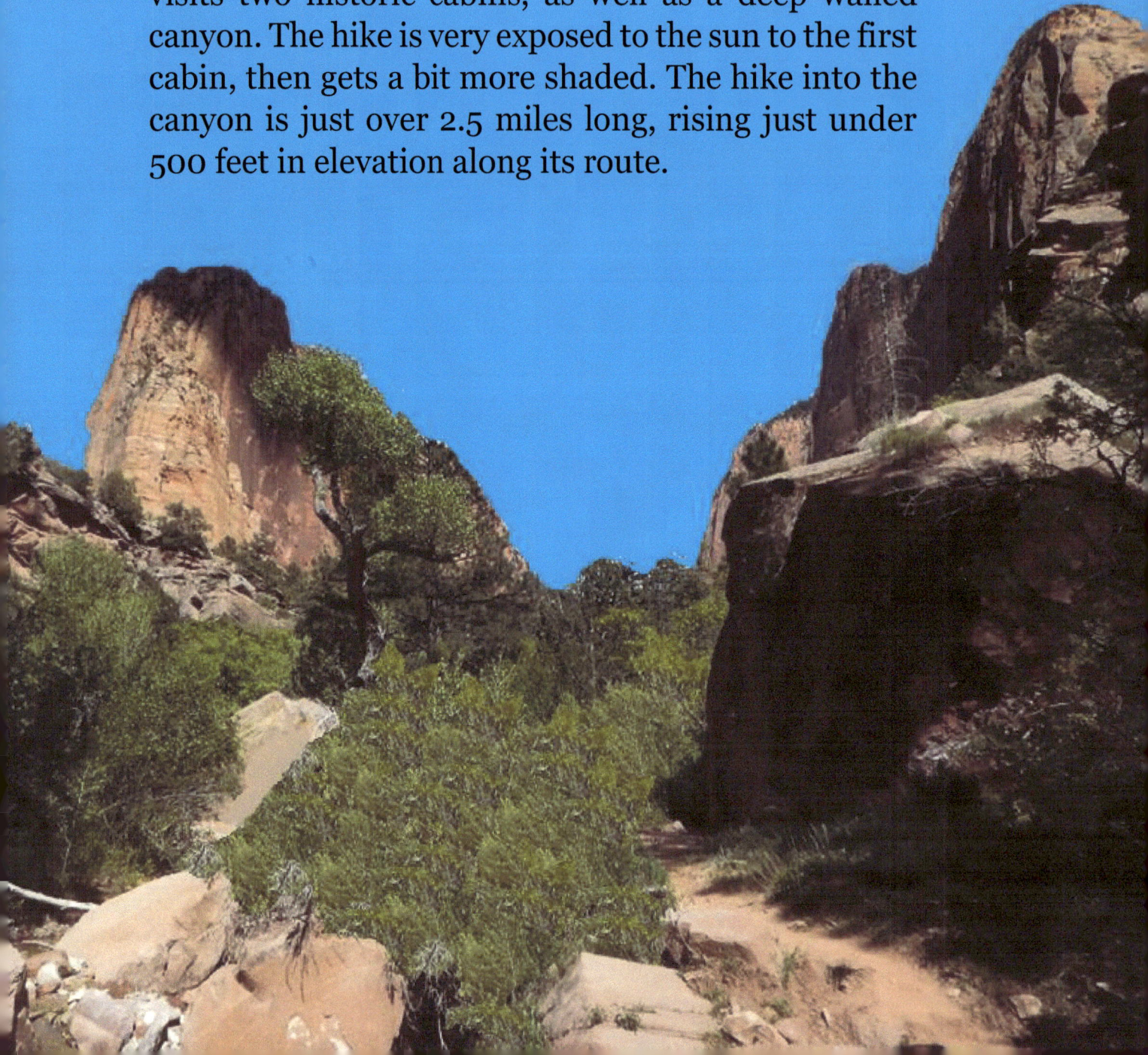

West Rim Trail. Fourteen miles of incredible scenery rivaling the best day hikes. From the West Rim Trailhead and through Potato Hollow, eventually rising 1200 feet onto the rim overlooking Great West Canyon, Phantom Valley, and Little Siberia down to Angels Landing. This is a great trail for camping overnight. It has plenty of campsites. You don't have to take the whole trail. You can turn around at any point. Day hikes are also available.

East Rim Trail. The trail heads up to the plateau with views of sandstone cliffs. A hike through ponderosa forest eventually leads to Stave Spring and the Deer trap and Cable Mountain. Or hikers can continue on the East Rim Trail and descend down into Echo Canyon towards Observation Point. The total trail is about 17 miles long. You can turn around at any point. Camping is also available.

Checkerboard Mesa are two iconic 6,520-foot-tall Sandstone mountains located in Zion National Park. The horizontal lines come from erosion. The rock gets sand blasted away from the high winds that funnel around the face of the mountain. The vertical lines are caused by expansion and contraction. The face gets hot during the day and cools at night. Causing cracks in the face of the mountain.

The 2.0-mile Kayenta Trail follows the Virgin River before ascending down an easy trail into the lower and upper Emerald pool trails. This hike offers panoramic views of Zion Canyon along the way. You can either return on the same trail or make a loop using one of the Emerald Pools trails. Kayenta Trail is in the most visited part of the park. Fairly easy trail with awesome views of Zion Canyon.

Pine Creek Waterfall is a lesser known trail for families. It is 1/3 of a mile and leads to the beautiful waterfall. During warmer months people wade in the pool below the falls. It is a short trail, but there may be some stream crossing and rock climbing involved to reach the waterfall. There are also a couple other ponds you can picnic at or swim in.

Orderville Canyon is a canyoneering trail for more experienced hikers. Most visitors will require a local guide or experienced climbing partner with the correct gear to complete it safely. This 12.3-mile slot canyon hike is a good adventure for both beginning and experienced canyoner's.

Many Pools Trail is made up of a pair of drainages with fascinating pothole formations. This 2.3-mile roundtrip hike is also easy enough for children to enjoy. The trail follows a natural drainage uphill, a little over a mile. It ends when the canyon narrows at the pools. But use your best judgement as this is not an official trail and is not marked very well. Great solitude hike with awesome views of the canyon.

La Verkin Creek trail. This trail passes by open canyons and cliffs while it travels along Timber Creek. After coming around the corner, the trail descends to the creek bottoms on a hard packed trail. Once at the creek, the trail heads upstream offering amazing views of Zion's red cliffs throughout the entire hike. La Verkin Creek is a popular camping, backpacking and day hiking trail. This trail is 11 miles in length from end-to-end

The Sand Bench loop Trail is an easy 3-mile roundtrip hike. The Sand Bench Trail is used by hikers and horseback riders. This trail is amazing. You get views of iconic mountains, a lovely bridge, and a stream filled with frogs and tadpoles in the spring and summer. The trail can also lead you over the top of a landslide that happened over 8 thousand years ago, and it formed a lake. The only downfall is, the trail is also used by horses and what they like to drop along the way.

The Grotto Trail is an easy, 1.0-mile round trip hike that connects the Zion Lodge and to the Grotto picnic area. This relatively flat and shaded hike is good for a leisure walk in the park. The Grotto Trail stays at the canyon floor so there is no hiking up hill and offers awesome views of the canyon walls.

Kolob Arch is the second longest arch in the world. It is 287 feet long and 75 feet thick. You can't stand directly under the arch, because at some point they think it will collapse. But the trail leads to some great viewpoints of the arch. It's cool how nature can create such fantastic rock formations like an arch. There are a couple different hikes to the arch that are long hikes. Many people make it a 2-day event and camp overnight.

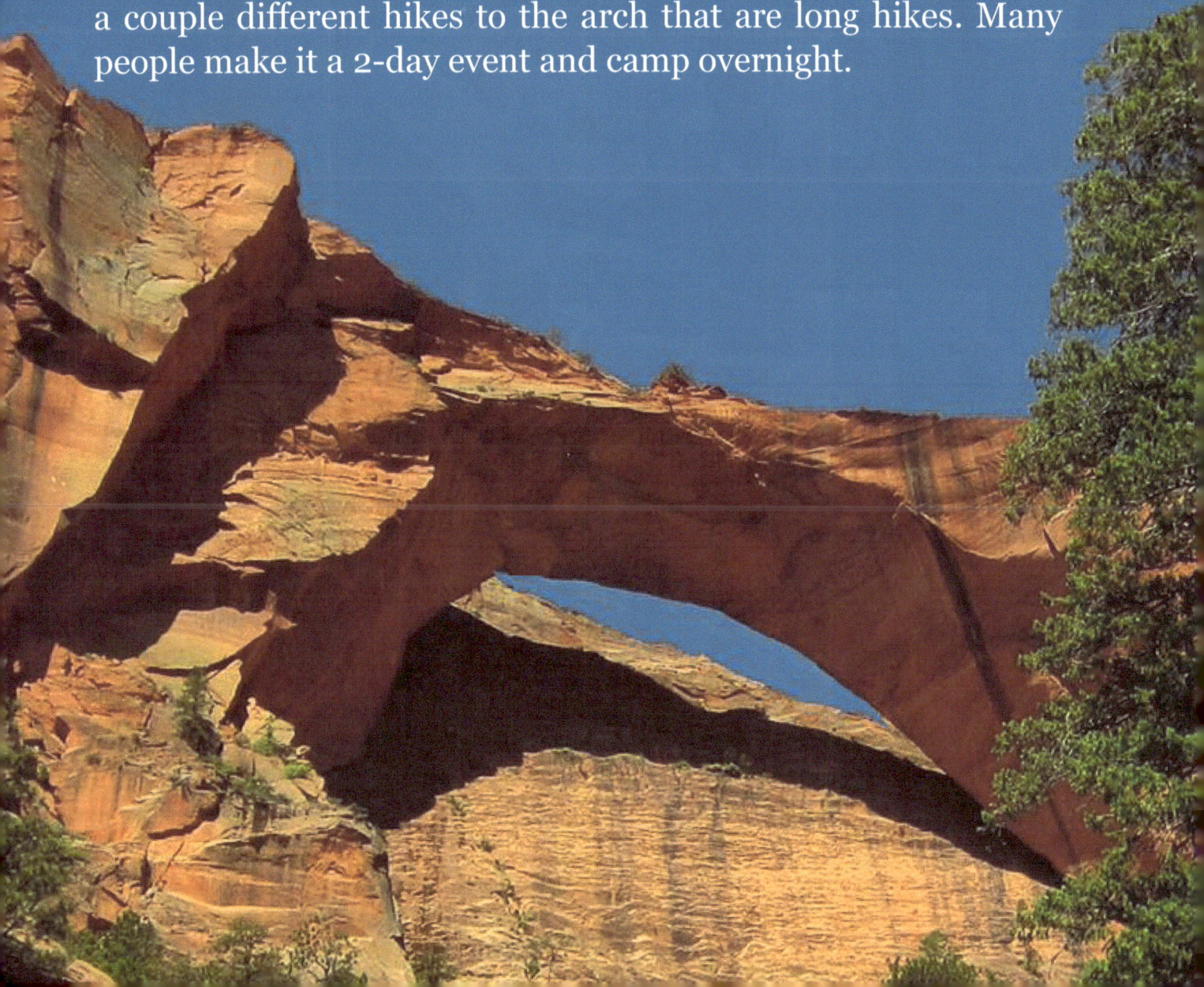

The Wildcat Canyon Trail is an easy-to-follow. It's a fairly level trail that makes for a nice hike. The round-trip hike is around 11 miles and could take up to 7 hours. You will enjoy views of the forested areas, the great west canyon, several wildflower meadows, and awesome views of the inspiring Cliffs of the wildcat canyon. Walking in the shadow of soaring walls can be an unforgettable wilderness experience.

The Timber Creek Overlook Trail is a short, 1.1-mile out-and-back trail. It is an easy trail that follows a rocky ridge with minimal elevation gain. Making it perfect for a short walk to a stunning viewpoint. At the overlook, you'll be rewarded with awesome views of many surrounding Mountains. Look to the south on the far horizon and you may see Mount Trumbull, 100 miles away at the north rim of the Grand Canyon.

The East Temple is 7,709 feet tall and has a summit composed of Navajo Sandstone. The East Temple is a spectacular landmark in Zion that can be seen either up close or at a distance. You can hike there via the East temple saddle trail. It's a 3-5 hour hike with a lot of rock scrambling to get there with some great views of the Upper East Canyon.

The Chinle trail is the only official trail in the southwest desert section of Zion. The terrain rolls over hills and dips into dry washes. It offers rarely seen perspectives of the landscape. This is the best view you can get of the fortress-like walls of Mount Kinesava, the prominent peak seen when driving to Zion Park from the south. Mount Kinesava is 7,285-feet tall. The trail is 8 miles long, one way. It is a desert trail, so it's hot. If you attempt this hike, bring plenty of water.

Some fun facts. The first Mormon pioneers arrived in the area in the late 1800s. They named the area Zion, which is ancient Hebrew for sanctuary or refuge. There are over 100 miles of trails to hike. Zion is home to 79 different mammals, 291 different birds and 1 thousand different plants. It has one of the world's most dangerous views called Angels Landing. It has the 2nd longest freestanding arch in the world, Kolob Arch.

There are 80 mountain tops or summits in Zion. The tallest is Horse Ranch Mountain. It stands at 8,733-feet high. That's 1.65 miles high. This is a picture of it.

# Activities Available and Ways to Enjoy Zion

1. **Zion History Museum.** Take a free tour of the museum.

2. **Horseback Riding.** Canyon Trail Rides are available.

3. **Hiking, Backpacking**. Enjoy walking through the trails.

4. **Biking.** Rent or bring your own bike.

5. **Birding.** Zion is home to 291 species of birds.

6. **Camping.** Zion has several camping areas.

7. **Canoeing, Kayaking, Rafting**, on the Virgin River.

8. **Ranger-led Activities**. Join a park ranger tour.

9. **Zion Shuttle.** Take a shuttle tour of the park.

# Author Page

Billy Grinslott & Kinsey Marie Books

ISBN – 9781960612991

Thanks

www.ingramcontent.com/pod-product-compliance
Lightning Source LLC
Chambersburg PA
CBHW060852270326

41934CB00002B/114